LETTERS PART ONE

Carlos Whitlock Porter

LETTERS. PART ONE
Carlos Whitlock Porter

(c) 2015 by Carlos Whitlock Porter. All rights reserved.

http://www.cwporter.com

Front cover art by Georg Sluyterman von Langeweyde.

Table of Contents

Letter from Catherine Colohen 4

Note on the Difference between Fascists and National Socialists 13

Half-Jewish Pro-Lifer Demands Retraction and Apology 18

From Tony Cavanaugh, Ex-British "Intelligence" 36

Gerard M. on Soviet Atrocities 40

From a Japanese-American
(On the Chinese, Koreans and Hara-Kiri) 46

From a Former U.S. Intelligence Officer on Irma Grese 56

LETTER FROM CATHERINE COLOHEN

With Comments by Carlos W. Porter

COLOHEN: Your sad and pathetic attempts to refute the great evil perpetrated by the National Socialists would be almost laughable if the filthy and dangerous lies you promulgate were not so easily available to those who perhaps do not possess the critical faculties or basic knowledge to see them as the twisted garbage they are. How ironic that the Internet, hailed as the future of freedom of information, should also be open to spreading the kind of Fascist propaganda you have posted on your Holocaust website purporting as some kind of fact.

Perhaps you think that the many Jews who did manage to survive six years of German atrocities are all lying or sadly deluded? The eyewitnesses...

PORTER: What eyewitnesses? Jan Karski? Myklos Nyzsli? Filip Müller? Hendryk Tauber?

COLOHEN: ...who lived day in and day out in the stench of burning bodies...

PORTER: Crematory ovens do not smell or emit smoke; cremation in ditches is impossible; how many times do I have to say this?

COLOHEN: ...or watched lines of people disappear into "shower rooms"...

PORTER: Where is the proof of this? In any case, the "gas chambers" at Auschwitz were morgues.

COLOHEN: ...and reappear as bodies that fellow Jews were forced to load into crematoria?

PORTER: What Jews? David Olère? Filip Müller? Myklos Nyszli?

COLOHEN: Maybe you even consider the presence of such crematoria in the death camps to indicate a Nazi predilection for baking their own bread, rather than burning bodies of innocent victims?

PORTER: They were built to cremate the bodies of innocent victims of epidemic disease, dying at a rate of 200 per day. By the way, if the "morgues" were used as "gas chambers", what did they do for real morgues? Where did they store the bodies pending cremation, since the crematory capacity was far less than that alleged by Jews?

COLOHEN: What possible motive do you think the Jews have to stage the disappearance of six million of their number?

PORTER: How about creating a pretext for setting up the parasite state of Israel with hundreds of billions of dollars in goods, money, gold, etc. etc. extorted from a world rendered psychotic by propaganda? No doubt there are other motives as well, mostly financial. See *The Jewish Paradox* by Nahum Goldmann.

COLOHEN: Do you think these people actually went to sun themselves in Madagascar for the duration of the war and were alive and well the whole time? Where do you think that the hundreds of thousands of inhabitants of ghettos such as Warsaw and Cracow went to?

PORTER: See *The Dissolution of European Jewry* by Walter Sanning.

COLOHEN: Have you not read the accounts not only of Jewish eye witnesses, but also of that rare breed at the time, the morally outraged German such as Oskar Schindler?

PORTER: Swindler was a Jewish racketeer working for the Germans and who is buried in Israel. Is this really the best you can do? An admitted work of fiction?

COLOHEN: This German provided intelligence on the treatment of Cracow's Jews during the course of the war, long before the mass delusion of Allied soldiers at the liberation of the camps that you implausibly attempt to argue explains their "mistake" of labeling German behavior deliberate extermination. Are all the Allied soldiers involved in the liberation of the camps mistaken or lying?

PORTER: Mistaken, certainly. That they were capable of lying as well – and torturing defendants and witnesses into signing false statements and confessions – is proven by the evidence they fabricated in hundreds of trials. How about the Malmedy Trial? It's not the only example. Why not read *Massacre à Malmédy?* by Gerd J. August Cuppens; *Crossroads of Death: The Story of the Malmedy Massacre and Trial* by James J, Weingartner; *Innocent at Dachau* by Joseph Halow, or many other books? One of the accusations dreamed up by the testicle-crushing Jewish-American interrogators at Malmedy was the homosexual rape of the bodies of American soldiers after the Malmedy Massacre; this charge was only dropped by American administrative decision. Otherwise that would probably be a "proven fact" as well.

COLOHEN: Where are the owners of the mounds of art treasures, personal possessions,...

PORTER: The personal possessions of incoming camp inmates were disinfested, registered, and stored, just as they would be if you entered prison or the armed forces anywhere in the world; as for the owners, see *The Dissolution of European Jewry* by Walter J. Sanning. Of course, many people died; the existence of their possessions does not prove that they were murdered, least of all in "gas chambers".

COLOHEN: ...teeth,...

PORTER: See Document R-135.

COLOHEN: ...hair...

PORTER: Are you referring to the 7 tons of hair mentioned in Soviet War Crimes Report USSR-8, or are you referring to Document USSR-511?

COLOHEN: ...that the fleeing Germans left behind?

If the crematoria were for less sinister purposes, why did the SS dynamite them before they left the camps?

PORTER: The fake "gas chamber" shown to tourists at Auschwitz I was not dynamited. The authorities at Auschwitz claim it is authentic, but that the "gas chambers" were blown up. So was the fake at Auschwitz I a "gas chamber" or wasn't it? They can't have it both ways. If any of these structures had been used as gas chambers using hydrocyanic acid, dynamiting the buildings would conceal nothing. The other crematoria were probably dynamited because of Soviet propaganda use of the German crematoria at Majdanek. Auschwitz I was a morgue converted into an air raid shelter at the end of the war, then converted into a "gas chamber" by the Poles and Soviets. The holes in the roof at Auschwitz II were pierced after the building was destroyed. No holes, no Hoaxoco$t. See the *Rudolf Report*. The real question is why they did not destroy all their records and archives, which have survived intact. See the *Technique and Operation of the Gas Chambers* by J.-C. Pressac, and the many refutations of that illustrious but unobtainable tome by Jürgen Graf and Carlo Mattogno.

COLOHEN: The list of damning questions you blatantly ignore is endless.

PORTER: So is the list of revisionist books you could read, written by persons much better qualified than myself. Why don't you start with the *Rudolf Report*? The longer version was long available only in German, but is now available in English. The questions you raise are answered in hundreds if not literally thousands of books, and cannot be answered in the space available here.

COLOHEN: Matt Smith's poisonous rubbish...

PORTER: Who is Matt Smith?

COLOHEN: ...argues that it was not a deliberate policy of extermination that led to the millions of deaths, but German mismanagement of the camps.

PORTER: It was due to the Allied bombing of railways and pharmaceutical factories, bombings which included dropping phosphorous on school children, machine-gunning refugees, including women and children and farmers working in their fields.

COLOHEN: Have you both failed to read the documents issued by Section D in Oranienburg during the war on the treatment of Jewish prisoners and their intended fate,...

PORTER: Please be specific; in any case, Himmler issued an order that the death rate was to be reduced at all costs; for further information, please contact David Irving.

COLOHEN: ...or that initial declaration of Nazi policy, *Mein Kampf* itself?

PORTER: Please be specific; which quotation are you referring to? Either the Hoaxoco$t was so secret that there are no documents to prove it, or it was public, and *Mein Kampf* and public speeches by Hitler can be used to "prove" it. So which is it? Was it secret, or was it carried on in public?

COLOHEN: Do you not consider the Nazi's intentions to be writ large from the 1930s onwards, with the rapid increase in persecution and removal of civil rights for the Jewish population, Kristallnacht, the wearing of the star, segregation of schools, ghettoisation?

PORTER: The wearing of the yellow star was an alternative to internment. National Socialist measures were largely copied from the Zionists, with the cooperation of the Zionists; the Nuremberg Laws were written in cooperation with the Chief Rabbi of Berlin, and similar laws exist in Israel today. The Jews have always "ghettoized" themselves; indeed, Judaism has very aptly been described as a "ghetto of the mind". See *The Transfer Agreement: The Dramatic Story of the Pact between the Third Reich and Jewish Palestine* by Joseph Black, or *Flashpoint: Kristallnacht 1938: Instigators, Victims and Beneficiaries* by Ingrid Weckert.

COLOHEN: What do you hope to gain by denying that the Holocaust occurred? It is not the first time nor, judging from events in Kosovo and Rwanda...

PORTER: The refugee movements in Kosovo were caused by NATO bombing; the massacres in Rwanda were the inevitable result of the chaos caused by decolonization, i.e., a black population explosion and black rule. Note that Communist, Zionist, democratic and African atrocities against whites are not important. Why not mention the white farmers being necklaced in South Africa while we are at it?

COLOHEN: ...all too recently, will it sadly be the last that human beings seek to murder each other on a grand scale. However, to attempt to deny that it did happen is not only insufferably insulting to those millions that either died or survived to carry the horrors of National Socialism and its death camps...

PORTER: If they were "death camps" why did so many people survive?

COLOHEN: ...to their graves – are you seriously accusing all these people of lying? –...

PORTER: Many of them, yes. See, for example, the quotations from the *Black Book*. Others, no. Hysteria was believed by Freud to be a racial characteristic of Jews; hallucinations are a symptom of typhus. Most of the "evidence" I consider simply Communist propaganda; just look at the references in any standard work on the Hoaxoco$t, for example, *The Destruction of the European Jews* by Hilberg.

COLOHEN: ...but leads to incidents such as the shootings at Columbine High School where young men,...

PORTER: One of whom, Klebold, was a racial and religious Jew, the grandson of a wealthy Jewish philanthropist.

COLOHEN: ...addicted to sick Fascist web sites such as your own,...

PORTER: They were addicted to a video of *Natural Born Killers* by the Jew Oliver Stone, which they watched over and over. They were also addicted to a video game called "Doom". Violence is as addictive as pornography; both are produced and marketed by Jews for billion-dollar profits.

COLOHEN: ...decided to mow down thirteen innocent people.

PORTER: When the story first appeared, it was stated that twenty five people had been killed. Now the figure has been reduced to thirteen. What could be simpler than counting bodies in an American High School? This is an example of the inaccuracy of media reporting.

COLOHEN: Perhaps you applaud their actions...

PORTER: Of course not; I think it is a shame they committed suicide. Hanging would have been far too good for them, and the same goes for the rap-music addicted 13 and 11 year-old killers at Jonesboro Arkansas, who fantasized that they were members of the Crips and Bloods, a violent black youth gang in Chicago. I blame the Jewish-controlled media for these events; but I believe that the idiots who commit these crimes should be punished; perhaps by necklacing – a punishment popular among blacks. Poetic justice! It is time for rap-maddened, black-worshipping white people and video violence-worshipping racial and religious Jews like Klebold to learn the difference between fantasy and reality, even if they are so-called "children".

COLOHEN: ...and see no moral responsibility on the part of people such as yourself,...

PORTER: I do not control the American news media, advertising, and entertainment; I do not control video pornography and violent video games; I do not make hundreds of billions of dollars by force-feeding the American public with unmitigated, endless filth, most of it of Jewish origin.

COLOHEN: ...but then you are the one who seeks to defend and exonerate the disgusting and barbaric actions of the Third Reich,...

PORTER: How about the disgusting and barbaric actions of Israel while we are at it?

COLOHEN: ...so you obviously exist in some kind of moral void. Laughably, you think that pointing out the incredible methods of murder alleged at Nuremberg somehow makes them untenable.

PORTER: Makes what untenable? Do you really believe that the "steam chambers", "electrical chambers", "vacuum chambers", and the other obvious lies, most of them of Soviet origin, do not rather tend to discredit the Nuremberg evidence and judgment, even just a little bit?

COLOHEN: Unfortunately, this is precisely why the Holocaust will continue to live on in human memory,...

PORTER: No doubt, because Jews will produce thousands of books, comic books, movies, and television shows about their "suffering", often in admitted works of fiction. You can turn on the television any hour of the day or night in any country on the face of the earth, and there will always be at least one show about "poor persecuted Jews" and their endless "suffering" and "sensitivity". Don't you think this has gone far enough?

COLOHEN: I believe because the scale of their evil and the suffering they inflicted was quite beyond anything ever witnessed before...

PORTER: Why? The Bible contains 137 descriptions of mass murder committed by Jews on God's orders; Stalin killed 10 times as many people as Hitler even if the Hoaxoco$t is a fact; not to mention Communist atrocities committed since Stalin's death (see *The Black Book of Communism* by Stephane Courtois et al). Will you join with me in denouncing Communism? Or is that further evidence of my anti-Semitism?

COLOHEN: ...leaving us wondering how these could really be men, not monsters.

PORTER: The same question could be asked with regards to the Soviet secret police, which were always dominated by racial Jews, for example, Yagoda; was he a human being? See, for example, *The Gulag Archipelago* by Aleksandr Solzhenitsyn. How about Menachem Begin while we are at it?

COLOHEN: Attempting to mock these facts is not to make them suddenly untrue.

PORTER: What do YOU think of the "steam chambers"? Note that the technical installations were described in great detail; it was not a "rumor" that Jews were being steamed to death, it was a deliberate LIE.

COLOHEN: I would suggest that not only are you an extremely poor historian, you are also a rather sick and flawed human being.

PORTER: As one sick and flawed human being to another, I am glad to meet you; by the way, is Colohen a Jewish name, or am I mistaken? To what do I owe this great honor?

COLOHEN: I would advise you to look deep within yourself to discover why you seek to deny these events.

PORTER: The answer is very simple. It is called a love of truth – combined with anger at the destruction of my race, nation, civilization, culture, history, and my children's future, not to mention sheer disgust at the exclusive and obsessive focus upon Jewish "suffering", real or imagined. I have nothing against former concentration camp inmates, I think many of them were decent people, but they weren't the only people who had a hard time. Nobody was dropping phosphorous or jellied gasoline on them (except when the Americans bombed them at the end of the war, more or less by accident). German concentration camp inmates were well-fed, and enjoyed sanitary facilities, heating, and health care; they lived relatively well until the end of the war, although of course they had to work very hard (10 or 11 hours a day). Perhaps you can explain why some of them were actually OVERWEIGHT, even at the end of the war? In short, although I have nothing but respect for many former concentration camp inmates personally, I am sick of their horror stories, hallucinations, and self-pity. I once asked a Japanese-American how he felt about spending the war in a "concentration camp", and he said, "Well, if I hadn't gone in the camp, I would probably have had to go in the army, and then maybe I wouldn't have come back". Do you see the difference? The Japanese have dignity.

COLOHEN: Perhaps, as for most others, the sheer scale of the horror overwhelms you so you choose to live in denial rather than confront man's gross inhumanity.

PORTER: I am quite aware of man's gross inhumanity, are you? Why don't you read *The Destruction of Dresden*, *Gruesome Harvest*, *Execution by Hunger*, *The Great Terror*, *The Black Book of Communism*, or *Ta Ta, Tan Tan: The Inside Story of Communist China* by Valentin Chu?, etc. etc., not to mention many more recent books, like *Eye for an Eye* by John Sack, *Other Losses or Crimes and Mercies* by James Bacque? There are thousands of them, why don't you learn something about the twentieth century before writing this sort of thing?

COLOHEN: However, if you will persist in continuing to trumpet abroad these grave lies,...

PORTER: The website consists mostly of graphics: are you saying I fabricated the pages I reproduced from the Nuremberg Trial transcript? Please be specific.

COLOHEN: ...I would be interested to see this letter and your response to it on your web site in the near future – you deluded Fascist.

PORTER: This is the third time you have called me a Fascist, a word used almost exclusively by Marxists. Does that make you a Communist? A pinko? How about "Communist sympathizer"? Name calling is a game two can play, and it is a game that Jews are notoriously good at. In any case, the National Socialists were not Fascists. If you like, I will write an article on Fascism to help you perceive the differences (see pp. 13-17 of this book). One thing the Fascists and National Socialists had in common was a love of country; a love of tradition, religion, and the family; a desire for social reform, and opposition to Marxism.

This is a revisionist website. Revisionism is a factual matter, not an ideology. Most revisionists are technicians: engineers or chemists, etc. Everyone has something to contribute, precisely because it is not an ideology. Many revisionists are Christians who believe that it is a sin to lie about any nation or people. Others are patriots who believe that a false sense of guilt is destroying their nation, their people, their culture, and their religion. Others are traditionalists who believe that an exclusive focus on Jews is destroying all nations, all peoples, all cultures, and all religions. Revisionists include Catholics, Protestants, atheists, Jews, Moslems, leftists, socialists, and, somewhat surprisingly, very many former Communist sympathizers. A few others (very few) are National Socialists. Facts are facts. $2 + 2 = 4$ even if it's a "Nazi" who says so. Nobody calls you an "atheist" or "anti-Christian" if you point out that the Shroud of Turin is only 700 years old. Do you really want answers to these questions, or do you just want to argue?

Yours faithfully,
Carlos W. Porter.

November 13, 1999.
Updated September 15, 2004.

NOTE ON THE DIFFERENCE BETWEEN FASCISTS AND NATIONAL SOCIALISTS

(Written exclusively and especially for the delectation of one particular person, Catherine Colohen)

Strictly speaking, the only "fascists" are the followers of **Mussolini**. Loosely, the difference is that the National Socialists believed in the primacy of racial factors and deficit spending. The "Fascists" (and their various foreign imitators) placed little or no emphasis on race, were often hostile to racial doctrines generally and National Socialism in particular, and usually believed in a balanced budget.

When Mussolini was appointed Head of State by the King of Italy in 1922, Italy had suffered 1.5 million people killed or wounded in the First World War; a politically-imposed bread subsidy threatened to destroy the Italian Lira as completely as reparations were destroying the German Mark, but could not be abolished because it was politically unacceptable; 180,000 politically-appointed railway employees could not be made to work but could not be dismissed; production was impossible because the Marxist-dominated labor unions had occupied all the factories and refused to work or leave; large parts of Italy were almost totally uninhabitable because of yellow fever or rocky, infertile soil and insufficient irrigation; irrigation and swamp-clearing projects had lain unfinished since the days of the ancient Romans. Mussolini balanced his very first budget, and solved all these problems in a very few short years, raising the birth rate of the Italian people and providing them with employment. These are significant accomplishments, which made "Fascism" very popular, at least initially.

All fascist regimes built tens, perhaps hundreds, of thousands of units of rent-controlled modern housing – beautiful modern apartment blocks, the best housing the tenants had ever had in their lives. Examples of such housing may be seen in an anti-fascist film called *Una giornata particolare* (A Special Day), starring Marcello Mastroianni and Sofia Loren.

Similar examples could be adduced from nearly all other nationalist systems. **Salazar of Portugal** balanced his first budget after decades of "democratic" chaos (3 revolutions, 18 military revolts, 40 governments established and overthrown, uprisings, invasions, assassinations, insurrections in all the colonies, persecution of the Church, confiscation of all Church property, the expulsion of the religious orders which performed all the functions of a modern welfare state [in a country which was 90% Catholic], etc., etc.: "...on May 14 [1915], the sailors mutinied, shot the captains of the 'Almirante Reis' and 'Vasco de Gama' and bombarded Lisbon... the revolutionary committees nominated Senhor Chagas as Premier, but on May 16 he was shot at and [fatally] wounded in the train, on his way to Lisbon, by Senator João de Freitas, who was killed... On December 5, 1917 a revolution... broke out at Lisbon... the rebels entrenched themselves in the Parque Eduardo VII and their artillery opened fire on the fleet... radical sailors mutinied on January 8 [1918] and bombarded Lisbon... on December 14 [1918] President Paes was shot at the Rocio Station by José Julio da Costa, and died a few minutes later...At Lisbon, the marines and Carbonarios [armed left-wing extremists, similar to the *checas* of Civil-War Spain], in February [1919] demanded government by 'soviets' and the abolition of the official police. Severe street fighting and serious outrages occurred, including the burning down of a block of government offices ...in October 1921, the barbarities culminated in the murder in cold blood of the Premier, Dr. Granjo, the founder of the Republic, Admiral Machado Santos, and other prominent persons. The appearance of foreign battleships in the Tagus made an impression, and brought the assassins to their senses for a time... successive governments seemed to lose control over the finances. No government was strong enough to raise an internal loan, to revise the system of taxation or levy a war-profits tax... taxes were paid in worthless paper money, [while] the Government had to buy wheat and pay the service on the national debt in gold... the roads... deteriorated... the state railways [fell] into a serious state of disrepair, and, consequently, it [was] found cheaper to import wheat directly from the Argentine than to send supplies to the north of Portugal from the Alentejo [Central Portugal, east of Lisbon]...".

Salazar reformed the economy, balanced the budget, ran the country at a surplus for 42 years, invested the balance in national industries, public works, public housing, schools, near-free housing for university students, national industries, bridges, transport, and other internal improvements, without a penny of foreign debt. Salazar's system was based on the encyclicals of Pope Leopold XIII. One of his greatest accomplishments was to keep the country neutral in two wars which would have destroyed the country: the Spanish Civil War and WWII.

"While Lisbon isn't as affluent as, for example, New York City, one could see it lacked, in 1968 anyway, skid rows and wino habitats."
– James Earl Ray, *Tennessee Waltz: The Making of a Political Prisoner*, St. Andrews's Press, 1987, p. 86.

In Spain, under **Franco**, it is still something of a mystery where the money came from to run the country: as long as he was alive the Spanish paid almost no taxes. Yet it was the Franco regime which carried out all the public works schemes which modernized the country. It was Franco who created the nation's first industrial courts, social and labor protection systems, * unemployment benefits, widow's pensions, etc. The real so-called "fascists" of Spain and Portugal (the National Syndicalists) never considered Franco or Salazar "fascists" at all, plotted against them, and even attempted to assassinate or overthrow them on several occasions, for which several were imprisoned or banished (Manuel Hedilla in Spain, Rolão Preto in Portugal). Franco distrusted both Hitler and the Americans; Salazar was pro-British and believed in racial integration.

* The following is only a sample of *franquista* social legislation intended to protect workers and apprentices. All this legislation is still in effect, but its origins are never acknowledged. Note the dates. "Frente de Juventudes" = "Youth Front". Even today, apprentices are permitted to participate in paid camping trips, etc. as members of the "Youth Front" (presumably stripped of any *franquista* patriotic content). The original intention, like that of the Hitler Youth, was to get the youth out of the slums and villages and into the countryside, eliminate class prejudice, show underprivileged young people other regions of Spain, reduce infant mortality by teaching girls how to sterilize baby bottles, etc. etc. and so on.

D. = Decree, i.e., D. 6-8-38 = Decree of 6 August, 1938 (the Spanish Civil War only ended on March 28, 1939, with the occupation of Madrid)

Date in middle column = date of official publication in the Official State Bulletin (compendium of laws)

D. 4-8-38	6-8-38	Requires registration and signature of apprenticeship contracts in the Placement Offices.
D 23-9-39	5-10-39	Establishes compulsory apprenticeship in industries.
D 23-2-40	27-2-40	Establishes the creation of apprenticeship schools in private industries.
D-7-3-41	11-3-41	Grants permits to masters and workshop bosses to encourage apprenticeship.

D-20-4-42	26-4-42	On relations between apprentices, Placement Office and Frente de Juventudes, in application of Decree 6-21-41.
D-16-7-42	21-7-42	On the concept of apprentices.
D-11-11-43	23-11-43	On institutions dedicated to vocational teaching or apprenticeships.
D-31-3-44	11-4-44	On Apprenticeship Contracts, Title III, Book II of the Law of Labour Contracts.
D-29-12-45	6-1-46	Grants twenty working days holiday for minors.
D-27-4-46	30-4-46	On facilitating [the purchase of] overalls for workers below the age of twenty one.
D-2-6-60	23-6-60	Prohibits night work for minors below the age of eighteen.

It is a mistake to believe that these regimes were never popular; **Juan Perón** of Argentina was overthrown twice: in October 1945, 200,000 of his followers descended upon Buenos Aires and made the country ungovernable. Perón was released from prison, held elections, and won on overwhelming victory. Ten years later, he was overthrown again. From exile, he instructed his followers to cast blank ballots in the upcoming elections, with the result that blank ballots outnumbered all others. **Pinochet** has one of the largest political parties in Chile, even today. Pinochet held elections, lost, negotiated a return to democracy, and voluntarily left power – a feat of diplomacy unique in history. These are facts which can be verified by anyone.

Update August 2007: Anybody who doubts that Pinochet enjoyed (and probably still enjoys) considerable support can just go on YouTube and search for "homenaje a Pinochet", "gracias Pinochet", or "Pinochet discurso"; and you'll find a ton of stuff, most of it pro-Pinochet. On the other hand, if you search for "homage to Bush", "thanks Bush", or "Bush speech", most of it is anti-Bush. OK, so where is Pinochet now that we need him? I admire Pinochet for overthrowing the government, not a bad idea at times, not necessarily for anything he did later.

The Bible [Eccl. 3:3] says "There is a time to kill and a time to heal"; it doesn't say: "There is a time to privatize everything and a time to torture people".

It used to be considered self-evident that any nation requires its own industries and employment for its own people. It takes the genius of the Jews to "prove" that a nation can be dependent upon its enemies to manufacture everything it needs, while simultaneously flooding the country with unproductive foreigners.

[Sources: 1922 and 1928 editions, *Encyclopaedia Britannica*, 1966 *Collier's Encyclopedia*; miscellaneous other books and periodicals; privately translated contracts and legal texts.]

HALF-JEWISH PRO-LIFER DEMANDS RETRACTION AND APOLOGY

With Comments by Carlos W. Porter

READER: Dear Mr. Porter,

As a Christian of Jewish ancestry who is staunchly pro-life, I felt compelled to comment about the content on your Web site. First of all, I agree with you that many Western "democracies", including the United States, have become the exact mirror image of the Nazi society that the Jewish people have rightly condemned.

PORTER: What I actually said, taken somewhat out of context, was: "By some pathological process of psychological projection, our Jewish 'democracies' have now become the exact mirror image of the (largely imaginary) 'Nazi' society which they pretend to hate so much. If a 'Nazi' society is a society obsessed by race; in which every conceivable decision of public, national, and cultural life is dictated by some crackpot racial theory; in which genocide is routinely practiced, with millions of innocent victims, in an atmosphere of general public indifference; in which grotesquely cruel and unethical medical experiments are routinely practiced by quack doctors in the service of some commercial interest; in which the bodies of murdered persons are salvaged, re-sold and utilized for commercial purposes; in which might is right, and human life has no value; in which brutal and cruel wars of aggression are launched on the apparent whim of the moment, without declaration of war; in which government routinely spies upon its citizens; in which dissent is routinely crushed, books burnt, and ordinary people persecuted and imprisoned for the expression of personal opinions; in which the news media are tightly controlled and routinely censored, becoming a mere vehicle of ideological propaganda; in which the school system is perverted into a mere instrument of propaganda; in which the cultural achievements and religious traditions of thousands of years are routinely perverted, destroyed, and ridiculed; in which the infliction of suffering is a form of entertainment; in which government is by a self-appointed minority of psychotics, perverts, and criminals; then our Jewish-dominated 'democracies' are the most 'Nazi' societies in the history of the world."

Actually, I should have said: INVERSE mirror image. America is becoming a totalitarian state, but it is not a National Socialist state; it is a reflection of our own propaganda. The United States of Phariseeism is doing everything it *accused* the National Socialists of doing, but it does not necessarily follow that the National Socialists actually *did* all these things. See comment on "Human Soap" below.

READER: However, as my father grew up in Berlin while Hitler was in power, I must take issue with your description of Nazi society as "largely imaginary". I can assure you it was not.

PORTER: The Germany of the 1930s was an open society, and a very popular tourist destination. Millions of Germans, including factory workers, travelled abroad, while millions of foreign tourists cycled, walked and otherwise travelled throughout Germany; their impressions are a matter of record. See *Ordeal in England* by Sir Philipp Gibbs, pp. 110-128, 165-199, and the February 1937 *National Geographic*. Millions of other foreigners attended the Berlin Olympics. National Socialist achievements were the envy of the world. Many respected Germans have published highly positive studies of this period; see *Kriegsursachen-Kriegsschuld* by Helmut Schröcke, Verlag für Ganzheitliche Forschung, D-25884 Viol, Nordfriesland, Postfach 1; see also *Verheimlichte Dokumente: Was den Deutschen verschwiegen wird*, edited by Erich Kern. Those who disagreed with National Socialist policies were free to emigrate ("Germany – Love It or Leave It"?).

Zionists were encouraged to emigrate to Palestine and were allowed to deposit their savings with the government and draw upon credits to buy farm machinery manufactured in Germany. See *The Transfer Agreement* by Edwin Black. A secret referendum on policy was held every year, always achieving over 90% (95% in an Allied-sponsored referendum in the Saarland in 1935). Policies strongly opposed by the public and churches, such as euthanasia, were dropped. In 1939, there were said to be 50,000 German refugees scattered about the globe, out of a population of almost 65 million; 3 years after the creation of the Irish Free State, there were said to be 100,000 Irish refugees, out of a population of 3 million. Perhaps these statistics are not correct; I don't know.

At any rate, millions of Communists and unemployed were converted to admirers of Hitler because of the success of his programs: The only significant resistance came from a very vocal – but very small – minority in the Churches, and, in the form of treason, from aristocratic snobs in the officer corps; this latter group almost certainly helped cause the war, and then caused Germany to lose it: about half the generals in the Russian campaign, for example. In the early 1930s, my grandfather had two young German dinner guests, one of whom was pro-Hitler, the other anti-Hitler, who got into an argument.

The "anti-Hitler German" became very angry and pounded his fist on the table shouting, "Hitler will *never* be Chancellor of Germany, because *he is not a gentleman!*" Some time later, this same "anti-Hitler German" wrote my grandfather a letter praising Hitler to the skies.

We assumed it was because he thought his mail was being censored and he wished to avoid internment in a concentration camp; but it is also possible that he was sincerely convinced by the success of Hitler's programs. Millions of others were indeed convinced. This possibility is forgotten. My grandfather never replied, and we never heard from him again. No doubt this proves he was "gassed".

READER: My father told me of the book burnings,...

PORTER: If I understand correctly, the National Socialist book burnings were purely symbolic: ONE copy EACH of several hundred books was burnt publicly. Many of these books could still be bought in bookstores, but were not displayed prominently. The National Socialists were amateurs at book burning, as you should know. "Democratic" Germany burns books by the ton, literally. For example, 14,000 copies of *Strittige Fragen zur Grundlagen der Zeitgeschichte* burnt by court order; my own *Nicht Schuldig in Nürnberg* ordered burnt, the printing plates, stencils ordered destroyed, etc., even though the book was printed in England. More books are prohibited in Germany today than under Hitler.

There are 15,000 prosecutions in Germany today, every year, for "thought crime", the totally non-violent expression of opinion. It is a crime in Germany today to say the most obvious things, for example, that other countries had concentration camps, too. You can get five years for it. It is called "relativization" of the "crimes of the National Socialists". Virtually any German citizen or resident can be imprisoned at any time; so can foreign tourists. It is astonishing what they do publish, but at considerable risk; other countries are not much better. If "Holocaust Denial" laws are not "Book Burning", then what is? Jews invent and demand these laws; are you a hypocrite?

Despite the symbolic book burnings, very real censorship, and the emigration of a few traitors, most of Germany's best actors, actresses and producers (Emil Jannings, Heinrich George, Werner Krauss, Hans Albers, Otto Gebühr, Carl Raddatz, and, of course, Veith Harlan and Leni Riefenstahl), painters (Wolfgang Willrich, Walther Hoek, Herbert von Keyl-Hanisch, Oskar Just and many others), sculptors (Arno Breker and several others), woodcarvers (Georg Sluyterman von Langeweyde and Rudolf Warneke), engravers (Werner Graul), playwrites (Gerhard Hauptmann), novelists (William von Simpson) architects (Wilhelm Kreis) and even jazz musicians (Teddy Stauffer, Erhard Bauschke, Kurt Widmann, Heinz Wehner, Kurt Hohenberger) remained in Germany, producing thousands of modern masterpieces in only 12 years. Hundreds of National Socialist films are so good that they are still shown occasionally on German television; the last film released during the war, *Unter den Brücken* (*Under the Bridges*), about bargemen on German rivers, is so peaceful that you would never even dream there was a war going on (listed on the Internet as "one of the best 100 romantic films of all time"; available with English subtitles from www.rarefilmsandmore.com).

For examples of National Socialist art, click [Internet link]. For examples of Hitler's own art work, click [Internet link]. When Hitler became Chancellor, his paintings became quite valuable, far in excess of their intrinsic value, as a result of which he prohibited all speculation in these works. To me, this indicates a man of some integrity.

To "prove" that no country can be artistic without Jews, the "idealistic" American "liberators" burned every copy they could find of certain German films (for example, *Kolberg* and *Jud Süss*, both based on true stories (there is also a British version of *Jud Süss*, made in 1934, but nobody cares, because the British weren't "Nazis"), destroying thousands of sculptures, demolishing beautiful monuments and public buildings at a time when millions of people were homeless, burning millions of books, and depriving competent people of all employment for years after the war, or imprisoning them for decades, purely for their ideas. It's the same story every time America goes to war. *If this is "freedom", what is totalitarianism?*

READER: ...he witnessed and the disappearance of his Jewish neighbors, who used to come to his parents' home for dinner (my grandmother was a Jewish convert to Catholicism, so they had a number of Jewish acquaintances). When my father asked what happened to their Jewish friends, his parents exchanged guarded looks and replied, "They went away on a trip." It was a "trip" from which they never returned.

PORTER: This is a non sequitur, i.e., my cat disappeared last week, therefore, my cat has been "gassed". It is true that many Jews were interned, left Germany after the war, and did not return; others undoubtedly died. They were not gassed.

A capital punishment website has two articles on American gas chambers.

Do you see any similarity between these complex, expensive installations and the crude National Socialist "gas chambers"? The

National Socialist "gas chambers" cannot have functioned in the manner described. Same with the crematory oven capacities and procedures. Should you wish to pursue the matter, please enclose the following at your earliest possible convenience:

a) an autopsy report proving that one single concentration camp inmate ever died as the result of inhalation of cyanide gas;

b) an engineering report proving that the structures alleged to have functioned as "homicidal gas chambers" could in fact have functioned as such;

c) a chemical study proving that the evaporation rate and properties of Zyklon were such as to permit the gassing procedures described by so-called "eyewitnesses";

d) an engineering report proving the possibility of the alleged cremation procedures;

d) a diagram of the alleged "gas chamber" at Auschwitz II showing the exact location of the "Zyklon introduction holes" in the roof which apparently never existed;

e) a series of other engineering and chemical reports sufficiently refuting the questions raised by Faurisson, Butz, Leuchter, Rudolf, Ball, Berg, Mattogno, Graf, Irving, Weber, Crowell, Walendy, and many other people far more knowledgeable and better qualified than myself.

READER: As a member of the Hitler youth, my father was ordered to spy on his parents...

PORTER: I am sure this happened occasionally, but I would be surprised if it was general practice; National Socialist Germany was not Soviet Russia. In any case, what do you think would have happened in the United States if enemy radio broadcasts posed a real threat to national security during wartime? Let's not be naïve. Millions of people listened to these broadcasts.

READER: ...and report them to the government if they listened to foreign radio broadcasts.

PORTER: Listening to foreign radio broadcasts was admittedly a wartime criminal offence punishable by death by shooting or guillotine. There is nothing in international law prohibiting wartime governments from taking measures of this kind. Incidentally, spreading propaganda – the "circulation of enemy proclamations dangerous to the interests of the belligerent concerned" – bribing or encouraging soldiers to desert, etc. are "war crimes" punishable by death under international law. "Failure to report a felony" makes one an "accessory after the fact" under the laws of many countries, including the U.S., even in peacetime. It should be noted that Allied propaganda was only effective in Germany during the first few years of the war; from 1944 onwards, its only result was to make the Germans fight harder than ever, as a result of American "unconditional surrender" policy, atrocities by our glorious Soviet ally, and publication of the Morgenthau Plan to "pastoralize" Germany.

Just incidentally, before I forget, in 1994, the President of *peacetime "democratic"* Germany, Richard von Weizsäcker, publicly called upon children to spy upon their parents and vice versa and denounce them for "right-wing views". Germany also has a toll-free number which Germans may call to report each other for "right-wing" opinions. "Right-wing" means anything anybody doesn't like particularly, even if everybody knows perfectly well it's true. There's no definition. So in *actual* fact...

READER: He also told me that Nazism was as much an attack on Christianity...

PORTER: There were various currents in National Socialism, most of them compatible with Christianity if interpreted in a certain way. Probably 99% of all National Socialists were fervent Christians; there were only a few anti-Christian National Socialists, such as Karl Frank. Martin Bormann was anti-Christian, but never took any specific measures to prohibit or combat Christianity; Hitler was Catholic. Priests were forbidden from joining the Party; that's all. Heinrich Himmler was also a devout Christian, who said "anybody who doesn't believe in God is stupid". The Bible does not advocate racial equality and does not even oppose slavery. John 8:44 is one of the strongest "anti-Semitic" utterances in all printed literature, an inspiration to Martin Luther and Julius Streicher. It is true that National Socialism has a certain pagan influence, but the Catholic influence is probably stronger.

Update 2007: The German researcher Werner Maser has shown that Hitler was extremely well read in the classics, and that National Socialism is essentially derived from Stoicism. Epictetus, for example, taught that health, wealth and possessions are of no importance, and that virtue resides in the Will, which should direct us to abstain and endure. Hitler talked this way all the time. The Stoicism of the Renaissance was largely influenced by Cicero, whom many people still read. Whatever one thinks of Stoicism, it is neither pro- nor anti-Christian. Seneca is considered by some to have been a precursor of Christianity.

Hitler did not "start WWII" and Jews were not persecuted "for their religion". Most Jews are not religious, and, in the modern world, it is the non-religious Jews who cause most of the trouble. Jews were – and, throughout history, usually have been – persecuted for their *actions*.

The reading list in an article linked to by yourself includes Hermann Rauschning's notorious forgery, *Voice of Destruction*, aka *Hitler Speaks*, so perhaps everything needs to be re-examined. That is my point.

It is ironic, but typical, that the accusations made against Hitler, in this respect and many others, are in fact far truer of Lincoln, a man worshipped by most Americans as a virtual saint; see, for example, *America's Caesar* by Greg Loren Durand, 1,072 pages, and *The Real Lincoln* by Thomas DiLorenzo.

READER: ...as it was a deliberate plan to exterminate the Jews.

PORTER: There is no evidence of any "plan" to exterminate the Jews or anyone else. The only people with any "plan" of "extermination" were the British, the Americans, the Soviets, and the Jews; see *What to Do with Germany* by Louis Nizer, *Germany Must Perish* by Theodore Nathan Kauffman, etc. President Roosevelt laughingly drew a cartoon of a "castration machine" to wipe out the German race in accordance with Kauffman's suggestions (see, for example, *Nuremberg: The Last Battle* by David Irving). Historically, mass murder is a Jewish character trait, not a German one; the Bible contains 137 descriptions of mass murder committed by Jews on God's orders. See also *The Revolt* by Menachem Begin.

READER: Many people in concentration camps and Nazi prisons were Christians who had protested Hitler's atrocities,...

PORTER: Which atrocities are you referring to? Please be specific. Excuse my ignorance, but apart from the "Röhm Putsch", I really can't think of any. In 1939, there were a total of 22,500 inmates in a total of 5 German concentration camps (according to other sources, even less, 7,500); most of the inmates were Communists or common criminals. Most were released after about five months. Communists were released if they promised to stop attempting to overthrow the government by violence. The Communist threat in Germany was very real: the Iron Front had an armed membership of 100,000 men. There were at least a dozen Communist uprisings in Germany before Hitler came to power. One in Berlin alone killed 1,500 people. There were also a quarter of a million suicides, often of entire working-class families. The first concentration camps in Europe were built by the Poles in 1922 to imprison ethnic Germans. Concentration camps *are not illegal under international law* and were not invented by the Germans.

READER: ...including Detrich Bonhoeffer, a Lutheran pastor who had participated in a failed attempt to assassinate Hitler.

PORTER: Attempting to assassinate the head of state is a criminal offence in all countries. In the US it is a felony even to *threaten* to assassinate the President. This offence is interpreted very broadly, and many people have been imprisoned for it who probably never intended to take action.

READER: A dear friend of mine is a Polish immigrant who was sent to a concentration camp; he has the tattoo engraved on his arm to prove it.

PORTER: Insofar as I know, Auschwitz was the only camp to practice the tattooing of inmates; I do not believe the practice was general, *if it existed at all*, since many inmates were released after a few months. The transcript of the First Nuremberg Trial contains almost no reference to the tattooing of camp inmates. As for the Poles and Jews, they have published too many lies for my liking: see *Story of a Secret State* by Jan Karski (Karsky), pp. 348-51; *The Black Book: The Nazi Crime against the Jewish People*, prepared by the Jewish Black Book Committee, World Jewish Congress, Jewish Anti-Fascist Committee USSR, Vaad Leumi, Palestine, American Committee of Jewish Writers, Artists, and Scientists, 1946, pp 270, 280, 313, 339, 356, 364, 375, 378, 408; *The Destruction of the European Jews* by Raul Hilberg, Holmes & Meier, 1985, vol. III, pp. 795-6 (green spots); (the documents are mostly Communist "war crimes reports", "affidavits" and "photocopies", most of the sources are Communist propaganda). Incidentally I spent 9 days on a Polish ocean liner in 1973, and it seemed that about half the passengers were showing me their "concentration camp tattoos" and claiming to be "Holocaust survivors"; this was out of 700 Poles selected entirely at random, almost 30 years after the war. I don't believe it.

READER: He was in a camp reserved exclusively for Christians.

PORTER: It wasn't Auschwitz then, which camp was it?

READER: He told me the treatment there was so horrendous that many prisoners committed suicide by throwing themselves against the electric fence.

PORTER: This is a staple of Holocaust literature; tell it to the Palestinians.

READER: He also said that he saw fellow inmates burned alive by Nazi guards.

PORTER: This is a serious accusation, one which requires proof. Otherwise it constitutes the sin of "bearing false witness against one's neighbor". This kind of hearsay is the crudest kind of wartime propaganda.

READER: Another friend of mine, Hilmar Von Campe, is a former German soldier who fought for the Nazis in World War II. His experience as a victim of Nazi propaganda, which brainwashed an entire nation to devalue all human life,...

PORTER: I do not believe that "National Socialist propaganda brainwashed an entire nation to devalue all human life". Where is the proof of this assertion? Sauckel's *"Exploitation Speech"*? It's only an example, but it's a serious question. I reproduced the complete translation in my book *War Crimes Trials and Other Essays*. See also *National Archives Head Fakes Captions to Nation-Wide Poster Exhibit*, in the same book. How do *you* translate "Seuchenabwehr"? My dictionary says "prevention of epidemics". National Archives head Robert Wolfe says it means "extermination". What do you say?

In actual fact, the National Socialists had good relations with the Chinese, Japanese, Hindus, Arabs, Zionists, and South Americans, the French, Slovaks, Ukrainians, Hungarians, everyone, in fact, except the British and the Poles, and even that wasn't from lack of trying. Even the Czechs committed fewer acts of sabotage during the war than the Germans themselves. The Czechs were the only pro-Soviet national group in Eastern Europe.

Hitler's political career lasted 25 years, during which time he wrote two 500-page books and made at least 5,000 speeches (warning: the mendaciously-labeled "speech" of "39.08.22" on the site linked to here – and even marked with an asterisk in the link provided by yourself, as if it were the most important of the lot – is a dishonest translation of a famous forgery, L-3, while the speech labeled "38.09.26" has been mendaciously "edited" to distort the meaning. Over *half* of the latter speech is missing, even though it is not even very long: about 45 minutes. The first half of the speech throws a different light on everything, including the war, and, in my view, vindicates Hitler almost entirely – but they can't be bothered to quote it. OK. I'll translate it myself, transcribed off tape. And what's more, I'll provide the *full German text*). Hitler's speeches have been collected in two or even three different 4-volume sets of books; his sentence structure is long and complex.

There were also thousands of issues of official National Socialist newspapers over a 20-year period. Yet the only quotations ever cited to prove Hitler's wickedness consist of 3 short paragraphs (or even single sentences) taken out of context from *Mein Kampf* (the "Big Lie", "15,000 Jews held under poison gas", "a maggot exposed to the light"), 2 short sentences taken out of context from the above-mentioned September 26th 1938 speech on Czechoslovakia ("My last territorial demand", "We don't want any Czechs") and a single sentence taken out of context from a January 30th 1939 speech on Poland ("the destruction of the Jewish race in Europe"). All the rest are from proven forgeries (L-3, the Hossbach protocol, Hermann Rauschning) and a few notes from other people ("The victor in war will not be asked whether he told the truth", from Ra-27), etc. One must assume that all the other – quite voluminous – material is either exculpatory or innocuous, as indeed it appears to be. The term "Lebensraum" was used, as often as not, in relation to a demand for the return of German colonies, a demand put forward to be accepted or, most likely, dropped, as part of a peaceful political settlement with Great Britain.

The National Socialists did not use the term "Master Race"; that is American propaganda; sorry.

One really would not expect the Marquis de Sade, for example, to enjoy a reputation for unparalleled depravity based on half a dozen sentences from proven forgeries, and then to discover that he also wrote half a dozen totally innocuous books that nobody ever bothers to read. Surely there is something funny going on here.

READER: ...led him to become a champion for the rights of the unborn. I encourage you to visit his website, www.voncampe.com/.

PORTER: I have seen his website and I strongly agreed with him at one time, but if he believes in the "Holocaust", then he has been the victim of some brainwashing himself. Further, he seems to believe that the post-war expulsions, rapes, murders, and enslavement of up to 15 million Germans were in some way justifiable, which is unacceptable by any moral standard. The Germans did not "gas the Jews" and were not responsible for the war, on the latter subject, see *The Forced War* by David L. Hoggan; *1939: The War That Had Many Fathers* by Gerd Schultze-Rhonhof; and many other books. I agree most especially with von Campe where Augusto Pinochet is concerned. It takes courage to defend General Pinochet and von Campe is to be highly commended for so doing.

(Update May 17, 2005: The Von Campe file on Pinochet seems to have disappeared, and at present I find little of interest on his site – mostly apologies to Jews, etc. He provides no proof of any "Hoaxoco$t", that Germany started the war, or that National Socialism was as bad as he says it was. He hardly discusses the matter. He supports Bush in his "war on terror" and believes that Hugo Chávez is a "threat to America". I despise Bush and admire Chávez. *When was the last time Bush got 116 out of 120 seats in a fair election?* As far as I can tell, Hitler, Saddam Hussein and Hugo Chávez all followed somewhat similar policies economically; for this they had to be destroyed.)

But the same argument applies just as logically to Hitler. Of the two, Hitler is by far the greater figure, and was far more successful, until he was forced into war by the British and the Poles, with secret promises of American assistance. Pinochet was also far more violent, but he was lucky enough to have the C.I.A. and S.A.S. on his side until he was no longer needed.

Pinochet believed in privatization and the "free market".

According to Soviet archive documents, Stalin was planning to invade Europe with an army of two million men – 300 divisions with 24,000 modern tanks, backed up by thousands of modern aircraft – by July 7, 1941 at the latest. The tanks and aircraft were built in factories constructed on credit by John Deere, Henry Ford and thousands of other "free market" Western capitalists, including Germans, and never paid for. It is estimated that had it not been for the German invasion on June 22, 1941, Stalin could have overrun all of Europe in a matter of weeks.

Thanks, "free market capitalism", we really needed that!

See *Stalin's War of Extermination* by Joachim Hoffmann and *Are the Russians Ten Feet Tall?* by Werner Keller. See also *Icebreaker: Who Started the Second World War?* and *The Chief Culprit* by Viktor Suvorov (a perfectly astonishing writer), and numerous books by Anthony C. Sutton, particularly *The Best Enemy Money Can Buy*; *National Suicide: Military Aid to the Soviet Union*; *Western Technology and Soviet Military Development*; *Wall Street and the Bolshevik Revolution*; *Wall Street and FDR*, etc. See also *Major Jordan's Diaries*. Many of the atrocities for which the Germans were, and are, blamed, were, in fact, committed by Soviet agents provocateurs.

When all the initial Soviet, largely American-made, equipment was destroyed in the German invasion, it was replaced by the United States at a cost of 11 billion dollars (the whole war only cost 37 billion). All the Soviet missiles, fighters, and fighter-bombers built after the war were copied from German prototypes made available by the United States, the only exception being a heavy bomber copied off the B-29. The simple fact of the matter is that, far from trying to "conquer the world", the Germans saved Europe from Communism, and would have destroyed Communism entirely, but were stopped from doing so by the United States. Instead, we got the Cold War, Korea and Viet Nam.

I repeat: Hitler would have destroyed Communism – partly by force, and partly by converting millions of Communists (see above).

The Soviets were also permitted to purchase uranium ore in Canada, shipping it out of the United States, by air, at American expense, through Great Falls, Montana, allowing them to explode their first nuclear device in September 1949, with the help of atomic secrets supplied by German-Jewish or Russian Jewish immigrants. 54 years later, under the influence of 25 Zionist "neo-con" advisors to an American President, it was allegedly discovered that a 10th rate Arab state, already decimated by American sanctions, possessed "Weapons of Mass Destruction", so we needed ANOTHER war! It's not even a coincidence that *both Gulf Wars coincided with the Feast of Purim, a Jewish holiday of vengeance.* For American atrocities in the First Gulf War, see *The Fire This Time* by Ramsey Clark.

READER: At the end of World War II, my grandmother, who had tried to keep my father's Jewish ancestry a secret throughout his upbringing,...

PORTER: There are many good reasons for keeping one's Jewish ancestry a secret; a sense of decent shame being one of the most obvious.

Ever heard of the "neo-cons"? Jonathon Pollard? The Rosenbergs? The reason Jews were persecuted in National Socialist Germany was because they do not make loyal citizens of any country they have ever lived in. They did not make loyal citizens of ancient Egypt; they did not make loyal citizens of Poland or the Baltic States or Imperial Russia, or of hundreds of other nations or principalities throughout history. In the end, they didn't even prove loyal citizens of the Communist systems which they worked so hard to set up, which is why the Communists turned against them and Communism was allowed to "collapse"!

They do not make loyal citizens of the United States of America – the most pro-Jewish country in the history of the world – so how much loyalty could be expected of them in a system explicitly *critical* of them? That a certain amount of injustice is involved in such measures is inevitable; there is injustice either way.

READER: ...discovered that they were both on a list of people who were next in line to be sent to a concentration camp.

PORTER: Perhaps this is why 150,000 people with at least some Jewish ancestry served in the German Armed Forces (see *Hitler's Jewish Soldiers* by Bryan Rigg).

READER: Nearly a victim of the Holocaust himself,...

PORTER: This is a non sequitur; not all Jews were deported, and not all those deported died. 75,075 Jews were deported out of a total of 225,000 Jews in France; this is an official figure from the Serge-Beate Klarsfeld Foundation in Paris (*Mémorial de la déportation des juifs de*

France, no page number); most of these were stateless or foreign nationals. When they didn't return to Paris to be "registered" at the "Ministère des ancients combatants" as "still alive" by the end of 1945, they were officially listed as "gassed". Simone Veil, later President of the European Parliament, was thus listed, under her maiden name. Between 60 and 70% of all Dutch Jews were deported, but only about 20-30% of all Belgian Jews. The Germans never even deported all the Jews available to them! In any case, their labour was required for the war effort. Virtually all belligerent nations intern enemy aliens during wartime; it is a "belligerent right". By virtue of numerous international Zionist "declarations of war" against Germany, beginning on February 24, 1933, Jews fitted into that category very well. Instead, they were allowed to emigrate all over the world, changing their names like crazy (as they always do). According to David L. Hoggan in *The Forced War*, 15% of all Jews who emigrated in 1933-34 even returned by 1939! This is because Jews shared in the prosperity of National Socialist Germany, although they no doubt disagreed with the racial aspects of National Socialism. There were no gas chambers, and not one Jew was ever gassed. If you disagree, prove it.

READER: ...my father became a vigorous defender of the right to life. This is a legacy he has passed on to me.

In the interest of truth, I respectfully request that you retract any statements on your Web site alleging that the Holocaust never happened...

PORTER: Unfortunately, this is typically Jewish. You offer no proof, you know nothing of revisionist literature, you have apparently read nothing else on the site, yet you demand a retraction and an apology. When the Jews, Poles, Soviets, British and Americans retract their lies and apologize to the 15 million ethnic Germans expelled, tortured, raped and slaved to death after the last war, when the Jews apologize to the Palestinians, or the Iraqis, when the Jews stop dragging us into new wars to suit themselves every five minutes, well... in any case I have no "false statements" (see below) to retract.

READER: ...or that those who suffered under Nazi society were "imagining things".

PORTER: OK. Do *you* believe in the "human soap"? That's the title of my article, *Human Soap – American Style*. Did the Germans abort their own children, "harvest" the body parts, and sell them to the highest bidder? No; they subsidized the family. They encouraged marriage, raised the birth rate, created employment, and discouraged homosexuality and pornography. Thanks to a five-year starvation blockade by the British with a total of 800,000 deaths and infant mortality rates of up to 85% (many of them *after the war*, since the starvation blockade *was maintained for nine months to force signature of the Versailles Treaty on June 28, 1919*), followed by Versailles, the Great Inflation, and the Depression, the National Socialists inherited a generation of rachitic, tubercular children, mothers unable to lactate, and nearly seven million unemployed, yet produced a generation of healthy, happy enthusiastic children, mothers, industrial workers, farmers and soldiers.

Membership in the Hitler Youth (which was copied off the Boy Scouts and English boarding schools) was entirely voluntary until 1939. Probably 95% of all German young people joined voluntarily. If the "steam chambers" were a lie, if the "vacuum chambers" were a lie, if the "quicklime chambers" and "quicklime trains" were a lie; if the "electrical chambers" were a lie, if the "gas chambers" are a lie, then how many other lies are there?

READER: My family is a living testimony that this is not the case.

PORTER: Another non sequitur. Your father is alive, so that is proof of a "Holocaust"! If anything it proves the contrary. If there was a "Holocaust", why are there so many "survivors"?

READER: I would appreciate a response, along with an apology...

PORTER: Isn't that just like a Jew?

READER: ...for your false statements...

PORTER: What false statements? The site contains approximately 600 graphics of original documents, thousands of exact references and dozens of translations and articles. Which statements do you allege are false?

READER: ...about events that still cause my father great pain.

PORTER: Tell the Palestinians about "Jewish pain". Maybe they're interested, I'm not. It's hard to think of anything more contemptible than using self-pity as a weapon against the world, but that is the Jewish stock in trade, and has been for 3,000 years. See also *Jewish History, Jewish Religion, The Weight of Three Thousand Years, and Jewish Fundamentalism in Israel* by Israel Shahak, a Bergen-Belsen survivor and resident of Israel. Shahak offers some very interesting quotes from the Talmud while we are at it. See also *The Jewish Religion: Its Influence Today* by Elizabeth Dilling (hundreds of pages photocopied from the Talmud, in English, permitting every possible kind of filth and degeneracy (for example: sexual intercourse with girls three years and one day old, boys at least nine years old, *but not one day younger, bestiality*, etc. etc., photographically reproduced, with underlining. It is not true that these passages have been quoted out of context by anti-Semites. The same material has been posted on the

Internet with a search engine and index – in both graphics and html; see www.come-and-hear.com/.

I asked an Orthodox Jewish supporter of mine what *he* thought of these passages from the Talmud, and his response was that the responses of "sages" had been confused with the religious texts themselves. I say: what kind of "religion" produces "sages" like that? It's not just one example; there are hundreds.

READER: Thank you very much.
Sincerely,
[Name deleted].
June 2003.

* * *

Update: Astonishingly, this exchange of correspondence went on for months and we became friends. She was very interested in Fred Leuchter, Germar Rudolf, Walter Lüftl, Dr. Richard Krege, everything. It was something absolutely new to her. She is a Protestant convert from Catholicism, bitterly resentful of Jewish efforts to eradicate Christianity from American public and cultural life, anti-Israel, and opposed to the war on Iraq. After I explained that I was not accusing her father of lying, but, rather, of being mistaken about certain things, she even apologized for her initial attitude, saying "I can be fooled as easily as anyone else, and if I have been believing a lie all these years, I want to know it... I am praying to know the truth." She also thanked me for "forcing me to think long and hard about things I had always taken for granted". I sent her a copy of Karski's *Story of a Secret State* (which she said was "weird"), and she sent me a copy of a booklet about the Federal Reserve Board. Apparently she is a writer herself of some kind. I believe that anyone can be made to understand the revisionist point of view provided he/she is interested enough simply to ask questions.

Carlos W. Porter,
July 26, 2004.

Personal Note: The three German-provinces of Belgium (Eupen-Malmédy, Sankt Vith, etc.) were part of the Prussian Reich until incorporated into the Kingdom of Belgium without a plebiscite in 1919. Farm labourers in these provinces were never covered by any kind of social security system until the German occupation of 1940-1945. The Grand-Duchy of Luxembourg never had an income tax [lucky them!] until introduced by the National Socialists; the income tax code written by the National Socialists was still in use when I left Luxembourg in 1989. The National Socialist Gauleiter for Luxembourg, Gustav Simon, is, of course, insulted in all the Luxembourgish history books and newspaper articles, but in Luxemburgish tax literature he is spoken of with great respect. Gauleiter Gustav Simon was in fact the author of the Luxembourg income tax code, continually reprinted in a two-volume set of books, virtually unchanged since 1945 [changes to the text were indicated in footnotes], with the original introduction by Gustav Simon. I used to have a copy of it, because it was still used by the Luxembourg tax authorities.

It appears that, under the National Socialists, and, later, at least up until 1989, if they didn't believe the information provided on your income tax returns, they made you *swear an oath that you were telling the truth.* (If you are an American, you really have to laugh). Tax evasion was not a criminal offense (what this means, or meant, in practice, if it is true at all, is anyone's guess; most laws are not worth the paper they are written on, in any system, including our own. It is the *method of enforcement* that counts). This is the "Nazi totalitarian state" we are always hearing about. Compared to the I.R.S., it sounds almost like Heaven...

I also had a copy of the *I.R.S. Special Agent's Handbook*, made available through the Freedom of Information Act, and reprinted in Volume II of *Tax Fraud: Audits, Investigations, Prosecutions* by Robert S. Fink, with Stuart E. Abrams and Elliott Silverman, 1982, published by the Matthew Bender Co., 235 E. 45th St., NY, NY, 10017, and let me tell you something, there is *no comparison*. Nothing is more absurd than Americans bragging about all their "freedoms".... just search google.com for *United States v. Jack Payner*, 447 U.S. 727 (1979) and see what you think... not to mention thousands of similar cases since then.

Hundreds of millions of Americans constantly talking about their "freedoms", but they're all terrified of their own government. This is "freedom"?

America has been a totalitarian state – off and on – since 1861, with various patches of freedom here and there. These "patches" are constantly moving, changing and diminishing, like sunlight moving over a landscape on a cloudy day with a storm approaching; yet we attack all other systems, both past and present, verbally and militarily, in the name of "freedom".

See also: *The German Revolution* by H. Powys Greenwood (very neutral; very good discussion of the extraordinarily complicated religious problems of National Socialist Germany); *Into the Darkness* by Lothrop Stoddard; *Look to Germany* by Stanley McClatchie; and *Warnings and Predictions* by Viscount Rothermere (1939); Rothermere visited Germany and Italy many times over a fifty-year period and knew both Hitler and Mussolini. Rothermere will be discussed in another article, along with *Ordeal in England* by Sir Philipp Gibbs.

On the deliberate starvation policies followed by the Allies during and AFTER both World Wars, see:

The Politics of Hunger by C. Paul Vincent; *The Revolver Republic* by George Eric Rowe Gedye; *Gruesome Harvest* by Frank Keeling; and three books by Victor Gollanz, remarkably, a Jew and the son of a rabbi: *Shall the Children Live or Die?*; *Leaving Them to their Fate: The Ethics of Starvation*, and *In Darkest Germany*; see also *Other Losses and Crimes and Mercies* by James Bacque.

For a unique compilation of quotes by contemporaries on all aspects of National Socialism and the war, both before and afterwards, see *Witness to History* by Michael Walsh.

For a unique collection on the Jews as seen by history's greatest men, see *Anti-Zion* by Bill Grimstad.

A good collection of Hitler speeches in a cheap edition is entitled *My New Order*, available second hand. You have to read about 250 pages or so before you get to the really good ones. Also contains reviews and comments on these same speeches, quoted from major newspapers, completely distorting their meaning.

See also: *Into the Darkness* by Lothrop Stoddard. Best short and most readable description of everyday life of National Socialist institutions and legislation, and how they effected the ordinary person.

Hitler: Myth, Legend, Reality by Werner Maser. Most objective biography of Hitler.

Afterthought: In one of her messages, this person told me that she had been inspired by *The Hiding Place* by Corrie Ten Boom, published in 1971. The book is a novel often described as an autobiography.

This is admitted in the French and Dutch Wikipedia entries, but concealed in the English entries:

"Elle a raconté sa vie à John et Elizabeth Sherrill qui en ont fait le roman *The Hiding Place* (1971) (nl: *De schuilplaats*, fr: *La cachette*) sur les périples de la famille Ten Boom avant et pendant la guerre. Ce livre est souvent présenté comme une autobiographie."

Translation:

"She told the story of her life to John and Elizabeth Sherrill, who wrote a novel based on her story, called *The Hiding Place* (1971), on the Boom family's adventures before and during the war. This book is often presented as an autobiography."

At any rate, assuming the Jews she hid were members of the underground, or otherwise wanted by the authorities of an occupation government, this sort of activity is punishable by death under international law.

FROM TONY CAVANAUGH, EX-BRITISH "INTELLIGENCE"

Note: Reproduced exactly as received, without editing.

As an ex member of Army Intelligence UK, I would like to ask the following question, from a military point. The questions are;
  if the Germans were not responsible for the Holocaust, who faked it.
  Who : persons responsible, to produce such a believable hoax, you would need at most members of the intelligence community, are we to believe that MI6 MI5, Army Intelligence, the French Secret Service, the NKVD, SPECTRA the GRU, the OSS Military Intelligence USArmy, and another number of organizations got together?
  If they did then it must have been some operation, and a degree of co-operation, that we could not achieve in the same unit. But let us agree that they did co-operate.
  WHY : to keep the Germans down, crush the white race, of course we must ignore the fact that with the end of the war in Germany the Asian war was still being fought. Nevertheless, this was the policy until the cold war broke out as predicted by Reich leaders. The first aim of Churchill's was to destroy German hegemony in Europe. when this was done, he immediately tried to train his sights upon Russia, but was voted out of office.
  While we can, the military authorities at the time didn't. To the top military, and members of the intelligence of the USA UK and France the battle lines were being redrawn in Asia. And I am not talking about Japan.
  We had neither the resources the time and the talent to waste on producing a hoax, But these were POLITICAL, and not military decisions. We had a empire to keep, the French had a empire to keep, and the USA had communism to keep at bay. However, the USA was all in favor of retaining the Soviets as their valiant allies until the Soviets revealed their true faces to American politicians, whose common sense had been effaced by Roosevelt's foreign policy of appeasement to the Soviets.
  In fact from an economic and military point of view it was important for Germany to be rebuilt and rearmed as quickly as possible

to counter the Soviet threat in Europe, therefore allowing us to fight them and their proxy allies in Africa, the Middle East and Asia.

You may ignore the Last 40 years of War with the Communist's, but as I took part I wont. So explain to me why various NATO Intelligence agencies while fighting a clandestine war, and it was a war, spent time effort and resources co-operating (I use the word co-operation loosely seeing attempts at co operation first hand), with the enemy, in creating a myth in order to destroy one of our closest and strongest NATO allies. From both a military and intelligence point of view it just doesn't make sense.

REPLY TO TONY CAVANAUGH
BY CARLOS W. PORTER

If I understand Mr. Cavanaugh's letter correctly – it is almost incoherent, and in places entirely so – his contention is that the lie of the gas chambers (which was a "proven fact" embedded in concrete by 1947 at the latest) cannot possibly have been a lie at all, because of the 40 years of so-called anti-Communist activity which allegedly came AFTERWARDS. I love this kind of logic; I just love it.

Ignoring the chronological non sequitur implied in this objection, may I respectfully suggest that Mr. Cavanaugh read the following books:

- *How the Far East Was Lost* by Anthony Kubek,
- *The Roosevelt Myth* by John T. Flynn,
- *While You Slept: Our Tragedy in Asia and Who Made It* by John T. Flynn
- *Roosevelt's Road to Russia* by George N. Crocker,
- *Are The Russians Ten Feet Tall?* by Werner Keller,
- *The Best Enemy Money Can Buy* by Anthony C. Sutton,
- *National Suicide: Military Aid to the Soviet Union* by Anthony C. Sutton,
- *'Twas a Famous Victory* by Benjamin Colby, and
- *None Dare call it Treason – 25 Years Later* by John Stormer –

all easily available second hand, along with hundreds of other excellent books and periodicals.

May I submit that the United States and Britain have never been anti-Communist? WWII was provoked by the United States and Britain for the sole purpose of destroying the two principal anti-Communist countries in the world, creating a void which could be filled by the

Communists. In return for declaring war on Japan the day after Hiroshima, the Soviet Union – the greatest mass-murderer and mass-enslaver in history – was given half of Europe, half of Asia, 800 million dollars worth of Japanese military equipment in Manchuria, the Kurile and Sakhalin Islands, and was deliberately built up into a major industrial and military power, all by the United States.

The Soviets were given 3 votes in the U.N, as against only one for the United States, plus a veto on the Security Council. Jewish immigrants of Russian and German origin – Greenglass, Gold, Sobel, Fuchs, Abel, the Rosenbergs, etc. – were permitted to steal American atomic secrets and transmit them to the Soviets; the Soviets were then given 40 years in which to develop their delivery systems with impunity, along with 80 billion dollars in so-called loans, "trade bridges", concessions, etc.

The result of all of this was the wars in Indo-China, Korea, and Vietnam. During this period, if you mentioned the Kulaks, the Cambodians, or the Berlin Wall, all you got was ridicule; but if one Jew wanted to emigrate from the Soviet Union, that was a worldwide moral issue.

It is all very well if you have a cushy government job "fighting Communism" with lots of bennies absolutely regardless of what the results are, but the average citizen or soldier expects something better.

Was Viet Nam an "anti-Communist" war? If so, then I have known just as many people killed "fighting Communism" as Mr. Cavanaugh, so please don't give me that one.

The sole purpose of the United States in any war between 1933 and 1989 was to fight just long enough to get a lot of people killed, and then give everything away to the Communists over a conference table. World War II was one example, and Viet Nam was just another. That's all. British ships supplied oil to North Viet Nam at a time when Britain was denying oil to Rhodesia!

American pilots had to fly over British ships docked at Haiphong Harbor – not to mention hundreds of tons of arms and ammunitions stacked up on the docks – to bomb targets in the jungle which they couldn't even see!

Now with the "fall of Communism" – which has not "fallen" at all, it has simply changed shape and is now more virulent than ever – we are miraculously allowed to win all our wars (Iraq, Serbia), for the sole purpose of creating a vacuum to be filled by Israel and by American multinational corporations (many of them Jewish-controlled).

Communism has ceased to be an economic doctrine, and is now exclusively an anti-racial, anti-national doctrine, Jewish-controlled as ever, a prime component of which is the lie of the German "gas chambers". Nothing else has changed. I preferred Communism the way it was. One could respect a Communist like Ho-Chi-Mihn. Old-style Communists were prepared to work and study, to plan long-term, to submit to discipline, to take risks. One cannot respect the motley coalition of human flotsam and jetsam who are the Marxists of today. Any decent Communist country would confine them to work camps, to the immense benefit of the world at large.

What Mr. Cavanaugh says about "protecting the colonial empires" makes me laugh. Has he forgotten the Belgian Congo, Katanga, Rhodesia? Which Western leaders does Mr. Cavanaugh consider "anti-Communist"? Truman? Eisenhower? Kennedy? Johnson? Macmillan? Harold Wilson? Mendes France? De Gaulle?

I don't have time to write hundreds of pages in reply to something like this. When I read letters like Mr. Cavanaugh's I feel like I am receiving e-mail from another planet. Maybe it was Bill Clinton who chopped down the cherry tree and said "Father, I cannot tell a lie".

Carlos W. Porter,
November 16, 1999.

GERARD M. ON SOVIET ATROCITIES

Note: Reproduced exactly as received, without editing.

dear sir,
i am a pure blooded aryan ,nordic young male actually born in Australia now residing in tampa florida. i just want to say that i absoulty was interested in what you had to say,indeed the western allies did much wrong,but the russians were at another level of depravity,those hordes of slavic scumbags raped my blood,the poor defensless women were raped by these russian swine. more time needs to be addressed reporting on the crimes of the russians instead of pointing the finger at the U.S.A. or britian. what they[western allies] did was not even half a percent of what the russians did.
gerard m.

REPLY FROM CARLOS W. PORTER

The Russian-American-British-Polish-Czech atrocity score is fairly even all around, with the Americans bearing the greatest ultimate responsibility of all.

Bear in mind that the U.S.A. had sole possession of the A bomb in 1945 and could have kept the Russians out of Eastern Europe entirely if they had wished; they could have destroyed Communism and replaced it with any system they wanted. [In actual fact, if it weren't for the United States, there wouldn't have been any Communism to start with.]

Instead they implemented personal agreements signed by Roosevelt and Truman without any Congressional authority, agreements which were totally illegal under all international law, not to mention American Constitutional law.

Nobody forced the Americans to dump millions of people in holes in the ground, without shelter or latrines, in violation of the Geneva and Hague Conventions, for 8 or 9 months *after the war*, while destroying uneaten GI rations and returning 13 million food packets to the Red Cross, each of them sufficient to enable an adult to live for 30 days. Bear in mind that it was the British and Roosevelt who provoked the war to start with; the Poles were simply pawns.

It is easy to bash the Russians because they have very poor credibility and are very poor forgers; they make an easy target; but ultimately it is the Americans and the British who brought about the situation and made it all possible from A to Z. This is true whether Americans like it or not.

I emphasized the Communist origin of the Hoaxoco$t tales partly because it is a very easy method of attack; but it is certainly not a complete explanation. The full story would be far too complex to fit on one website.

The so-called "Civil War" is another example ("Lincoln freed the slaves", etc.). The simple fact is that slavery was never abolished in the North until after Lincoln was killed. The issue was to strengthen the power of the Federal Government at the expense of the states, retain a captive market for Northern manufactured goods, and force Southerners to pay 90% of all national taxes. Sound familiar?

For example, the bombardment of Fort Sumter was deliberately provoked by Lincoln to cause a war; the Confederates had no choice. In the face of an approaching Federal fleet, they either had to take the fort and protect the city, or they had to wait for the fleet to reinforce the fort and destroy the city. This was in violation of all public promises made by both Lincoln and his Secretary of War, Steward. "Slavery" was only tossed in two years later.

All these "ideological crusades" are simply pretexts.

The sinking of the Lusitania in 1914; the deliberate provocation of mass civilian population bombing by the British in 1940, in which a million civilians were burnt to death, were both plots to get America into a war, just like the explosion of the USS Maine in 1898, which I personally believe to have been destroyed by an American time bomb (the wreckage was raised in 1908 and proven to have been caused by an internal explosion, after which it was towed out to sea and sunk in deep water so nobody could ask any more questions – it's called "destruction of evidence").

The manufacture of these incidents is a consistent pattern. Winston Churchill was talking to Charles de Gaulle in the backyard of Chequers, Churchill's home; Churchill shook his fist at the sky and shouted, "So they won't come!", referring to German bombers! De Gaulle said, "Are you in such a hurry to see your towns smashed to bits?" Churchill said, "You see, the bombing of Oxford, Coventry, Canterbury will cause such a wave of indignation in the United States they'll come into the war".

It's in de Gaulle's autobiography. It's quoted in *Roosevelt's Road to Russia* by George N. Crocker, Henry Regnery Company, Chicago,

1959, p. 166-8 (see innumerable footnotes in Chapter X). Crocker was a Law Professor, Law School Dean, a practitioner in the State and Federal courts, an Assistant United States Attorney, a graduate of Stanford University, Harvard Law School, a Member of Phi Beta Kappa and the Bar of California, and a former U.S. Army officer. Crocker knew history, and he knew the Law.

Human life means no more to our "democratic" leaders today it did to Genghis Khan. In fact, the system is even more corrupt, because to be leader of a Mongol horde, one had to be a man of proven ability, and, presumably, look after the interests of the Mongols. So please don't tell me we wouldn't fake a few "terrorist attacks" to start a war for Israel.

The Communists didn't give *themselves* half of Europe and Asia, they were promised those areas by American Presidents *without any constitutional or legal authority whatsoever*.

If the Russians raped 1.2 million women in Germany after the war, it was the Americans who made it possible. 9 million Germans lost their lives *after the war*. Why? Not because of the Russians, but because the Americans *permitted* it.

You might as well say Ariel Sharon bears no responsibility for the 2,000 murders committed in the Palestinians refugee camps of Sabra and Shatila in 1982, etc., just because he didn't do it himself, personally. The area was fenced off by the Israeli Army and floodlit night and day for 36 hours with exclusive entry permitted to armed members of the Lebanese Phalange (a Christian militia group paid, armed, and uniformed by the Israelis), in the knowledge that the Phalange would murder everyone in the camps, which they immediately did – for 36 hours, under Israeli floodlights, protected by Israeli roadblocks.

Ultimate responsibility is ultimate responsibility, even if other parties are involved with intermediate or instrumental responsibility.

I am a little bit surprised that you accuse me of America-bashing, since the title of the website is *Made in Russia – The Holocaust*, simply because most of the evidence is Communist propaganda.

I don't suppose it is remotely possible that Americans now consider themselves entirely above criticism because of the self-inflicted and/or at any event well-deserved events of September 11, do they?

"Remember Pearl Harbor" – not because the Japs did it, but because the Americans wanted them to, knew they would, and gave them no choice. See my article *Japan Was Provoked into a War of Self-Defense*, in my book *War Crimes Trials and Other Essays*.

Another example is the Alfred P. Murrah Building in Oklahoma City, blown up by Federal agents to destroy the militia movement and gain the passage of emergency legislation. The Feds have no respect for the lives of ordinary Americans or anyone else (just as one example, people were allowed to bleed to death while Federal agents removed explosives illegally stored in the building, etc. etc. etc. blah, blah, blah, how much do you want to hear?)

Fuel-oil nitrate ammonium is a blast explosive, not a demolition explosive. Believing that McVeigh's crude truck bomb could cause that much damage is like believing that 19 ignorant Arabs with plastic knives (Arabs who got kicked out of flying school, had no professional flying experience, and were not qualified to fly a Cessna or Piper Cub) could fly 4 different commercial airliners as if they were fighter planes, with all sorts of evasive maneuvers, after which much of the wreckage mysteriously disappeared (particularly, at the Pentagon), or that F.D.R. was innocently preparing to fiddle with his stamp collection when "surprised" by the news of the "infamous" "surprise" attack on Pearl Harbor.

These are complex matters, and I hope that you will have find the time to do some of the research required to verify the statements made above. The links are available on this website, featured as prominently as I could make them. I particularly recommend the Final Report of the Oklahoma City Bombing Investigation Committee (most particularly, the technical reports of the various demolitions experts). *

Perhaps part of the answer is what David L. Hoggan has called "The Messianic Ideal In American Education", or what Charles A. Beard called "The Devil Theory of War". Americans can do no wrong, because we are the avenging angels of a jealous Yahway – except where Communists, Jews, or Israelis are concerned, of course.

A few years ago, if you claimed it was even possible to win in Viet Nam, people treated you like you were crazy! Now we go around booting half the world in the groin from one moment to the next, without so much has a by-your-leave from anyone, and think nothing of it! The only thing that's happened is that the Jews have changed sides, that's all.

This is an anti-Nuremberg revisionist website, not a Russian-Communist atrocity website. Why don't you start a website of your own, assuming you possess the literacy to do so?

* The Report contains a very important disclaimer on p. 320: "We have never claimed that the federal government bombed their own building. That's merely a propaganda campaign meant to discredit anyone who tries to bring the facts to light". Unfortunately, that is precisely what the Report proves whether The

Oklahoma City Bombing Investigation Committee likes it or not. Don't get your information second hand off the Internet. Buy it and read it.

CONCLUSION

To me, there are only two possibilities: a) McVeigh was guilty, but was still framed, i.e., the FBI infiltrated the group, set off their own bombs to discredit the militia movement, then arrested him; or b) (much more likely but impossible to prove) McVeigh was a government agent, the government promised him the earth, moon and stars above, promised him the execution would be fake, he would be given a new identity, millions of bucks, plastic surgery, etc., luxury life in the Bahamas, or something, then betrayed and killed him.

Everything else is impossible.

Even a) is impossible, at least according to the official story. He rents a truck using a fake ID, but gives his own, real, address, in Decker Michigan, but without a credit card. No credit card is ever mentioned, the rental forms are never produced, no photocopy of the fake driver's license was ever produced, he sets off the bomb, which he is stupid enough to believe has actually done all that damage, is arrested driving without license plates, is asked, "Why don't you have any plates?", he says, "Because I just bought the car", where, then he names the city where he rented the truck! He is carrying a concealed .45, with a "cop-killer" (dum-dum) in the magazine or top bullet in the clip (it is not clear which) but does not resist arrest. The cop says, do you have any weapons? He says, "Yeah, I've got a gun. I've also got a knife" (a pocket knife). Then in court he never says a word in his own defense.

Sherlock Holmes said when you have eliminated the impossible, what remains, no matter how improbable, must be the truth. The fallacy is knowing when you have eliminated the impossible. But in this case what other alternative is there? I think he claimed he was implanted with a microchip that controlled his actions. I think that is scientifically impossible. But who knows really?

His execution, where he shows up ice cold and reads a poem that says "I am the master of my fate, I am the captain of my soul", etc., is all very well for Hollywood, but I don't believe it in real life.

Let's face it: If he had blown up a public building on some sort of secret mission in Iraq under the exact same circumstances, killing the exact same number of women and children and civilians, and had been executed by the Iraqis in exactly the same way, he would be one of the greatest military martyrs and heroes in history, and his execution would be considered a great crime, "judicial murder", just like the bomber pilots and navigators (a grand total of 2 each, I think), beheaded by the Japanese.

I don't believe it. I think he was an agent, they tricked him, and the execution was real. I think he thought he was doing a great act of patriotism by discrediting the militia movement so the government could move against "unpatriotic elements" and then they double-crossed him.

[Poem]

Out of the night that covers me,
Black as the Pit from pole to pole,
I thank whatever gods may be
For my unconquerable soul.
In the fell clutch of circumstance
I have not winced nor cried aloud.
Under the bludgeonings of chance
My head is bloody, but unbowed.
Beyond this place of wrath and tears
Looms but the Horror of the shade,
And yet the menace of the years
Finds, and shall find, me unafraid.
It matters not how strait the gate,
How charged with punishments the scroll,
I am the master of my fate:
I am the captain of my soul.

If you were about to be executed would you show up and read this? Hollywood.

No credit card, nothing. For xyz years since then. They should have photocopied the ID, the rental forms, everything. John Doe no. 2 disappears, McVeigh is arrested for staying in a motel room nearby, they produce that form, whoopee!

I tried renting a car, twice, with no credit card, in the 1970s and 80s, impossible, in 2 states. And why fake an ID then give your real address? Where are the forms?...

Carlos W. Porter,
April 8, 2002.
(somewhat updated)

FROM A JAPANESE-AMERICAN
(ON THE CHINESE, KOREANS
AND HARA-KIRI)

Japanese-American: What do you know about Koreans? I seem to be having a very hard time understanding their mentality. The (small) amount of study done on them is surprising considering that they're supposed to be one of the major races of East Asia. There's almost nothing about them in the 1911 *Encyclopaedia Britannica*. To me, they're just a bunch of morbid gooks bordering on insanity. It's unbelievable how obsessed they are with Japan.

I don't know if you heard, but there's a dispute going on now over a bunch of uninhabited islands in the Sea of Japan, the Takeshima islands, that are so small that none of my World Atlases even cover them. I have no problem with the Koreans protesting about it, but some of the things they do just sickens me. I don't know why, but they have this strong tendency to cut themselves. Everybody in Korea is doing it, an assemblyman from Seoul was just arrested today for attempting to cut himself in some government building in Japan. I just can't understand how such a person of high stature would be willing to fly to Japan just to cut himself over a bunch of midget islands. Do you?

Carlos W. Porter: No. But from the point of view of a Westerner the same thing could be said about the Japanese. I don't understand hara-kiri. Suicide, yes, but not hara-kiri. Not jumping into volcanoes, etc.

Seppukku (hara-kiri) is logical if you believe that the "ki" (life-spirit, energy or soul) is centered in the "hara" (belly), you dig, but really, one might try to make it a bit less painful... Anybody knows you die quicker if you stab yourself in the jugular vein or carotid artery.

Same with the volcano. Why not jump off a cliff? Why do you need a volcano? It's a fascination with self-punishment. As for Korea...

(**Background:** The 1911 *Encyclopaedia Britannica*, which this person mentions, points out that the Korean peninsula is a "dagger pointed at the heart of Japan": any country that dominates Korea will dominate the Sea of Japan and constitute a direct threat to Japan. After fighting two wars to guarantee the independence of Korea (the First Sino-Japanese War of 1894-95 and the Russo-Japanese War of 1904-05), the Japanese chose to make the country a protectorate.

Judging from the 1911 *EB*, Korea at that time must have been one of the most corrupt and backward countries on earth. The Japanese charted the coasts, built lighthouses, railways, roads, schools, clinics, telegraph lines, reformed the currency, civil service and court system, eliminated corruption and modernized the whole country.

There is no question but that they were much better off under the Japanese, but all they can do is express an obsessive hatred for the Japs, as this person very correctly says; yet the only concrete grievance I've ever heard about is that the Japs put up street signs in Japanese (presumably both languages)! What did they expect? Korean and Japanese are completely different languages. Koreans really are "obsessed" with the Japanese, while the Japs hardly even think of Korea. To me, this looks like an obvious inferiority complex.

In any case, the traditionally intense Korean hatred of Japan dates back to the end of the 16th century, when Japan invaded Korea to expel an army of Chinese, which had already conquered the country. The 1910 annexation was carried out peacefully, by agreement with the Korean government, which was apparently attempting to escape increasing Chinese domination. The Koreans have walked a tightrope for thousands of years. This is not the fault of Japan; it is the fault of geography.)

...Koreans are sadistic. Just look at some of the *hapkido* (Korean jiu-jitsu) videos on YouTube. They're the only martial artists who really seem to hurt their students. I'd hate to see what their joints look like at age 40. One of my wife's relatives was captured by the Japs and he said the Japanese weren't too bad, but they had some other Oriental race with them who were terrible. Who could it have been but Koreans?

(Big new story: anti-Japanese riots in China involving 5-10,000 people.)

China is a big country and let's face it, it's far away, so 5-10,000 people riot in China because they hate Japan, and it's a big deal? While they cover up worldwide peace demonstrations involving millions of people?

By the way, I keep hearing stories derived from Chinese propaganda, one minute it's human vivisection, next it's Japanese germ warfare. The chinks remind me of the Jews, in fact they used to be called "the Jews of the Orient". I'm sick of all their caterwauling.]

ON GENERAL DECADENCE

Japanese-American: There are some major issues with Japan today. I haven't personally encountered any of it because I don't hang around in those areas, but I've heard stories. The way some of them dress in public and act on TV is very unusual, weird. Just to prove how lost

Japanese society is, rap is the craze there. Not Japanese rap, but American rap straight from the hood. I can understand pop, but rap? I asked a kid once if he understood anything they were saying in the music and he told me it didn't matter. Crime rates are going up, suicide rates are going up, everything's falling apart. My mom once told me you didn't have to lock your house in Japan because the whole country was safe. Now that's just an illusion.

I agree with you on *seppuku* (hara-kiri), nobody I ask even knows why the ancient samurais did it. I'm curious to know as to who invented the practice and when.

Carlos W. Porter: It's a religious problem, Gustave Le Bon in *Psychology of Crowds* says that civilizations are born when they have a dream, no matter what it is, and are destroyed when they lose the dream. In the Orient, it was Shintoism and Buddhism. I'm a traditionalist.

Japanese-American: What a hole we're burying ourselves in. Society is completely worthless. I don't understand it at all, why are they doing this? Is it to destroy our sense of community? And for what? I'm sick of all this. All of this talk about the "American Dream" just to justify millions of illegals. It's suicide. One thing I don't understand still is why fascism was erroneous. It seems to have been very efficient, especially compared to that of countries today.

Carlos W. Porter: It occurs to me that the industrialized nations are treating their own populations like the slave populations in South America. It was cheaper to import adult slaves than to feed and clothe their children until they were old enough to work. The average life expectancy of a slave in Brazil or Cuba was, for a time, 9 years (because of disease, due to the climate, not because they were worked to death) after which they just imported more. The American South was the only exception. It's the same mentality, cheap labor, a quick buck, even if the slaves are well-treated (as they were in the South). These countries were perfectly correct in saying that the prosperity of their economies depended on slave labor (indeed much of the economy of the world, indirectly, since manufactured goods of all kinds were traded to Africans in return for slaves). So today we import adult immigrants (slaves) because it's less trouble than doing our own work and having our own children. It's the implosion of the industrialized, urbanized way of life, and even worse, plus all the factors that destroyed Rome. It's destroyed every civilization in history (see *Why Civilizations Self-*

Destruct by Elmer Pendell, *March of the Titans: A History of the White Race* by Arthur Kemp, etc.). There is also an article in the 1928 *Encyclopaedia Britannica* about this: when people reach a certain standard of living they quit having children and are destroyed by their lower classes, slaves, or barbarian invaders. At least the Germanic tribes were white. I've never believed in progress, it's a delusion. Which is more important, your race, or your economy?

It all reminds me of the Japanese soldier that spent 28 years in the jungles of the Pacific after the war and then saw Japanese girls in miniskirts drinking Coca Cola and said, "They can't be Japanese". It's the fault of the Americans. Of course, numbers of people aren't important if the quality stays the same, but that won't happen.

It's the capitalistic mentality of short-term profit and expediency, pleasure, the antithesis of traditionalist Japan, or indeed of almost all past world societies. No society has ever had such values. Somebody told me, "We won't have to worry about that, our children will". It's not normal. It's unprecedented. To me, the only alternative is National Socialism, but for that you'd need a total human regeneration, like a religious conversion, the lion lying down with the lamb. The Jews will run the world into the ground first.

If the Americans hadn't sided with China and destroyed Japan, they wouldn't have needed to limit their population, and wouldn't have gotten into the habit of aborting all their children, etc. 2/3 of all children were aborted, even 35-40 years ago, or something, even when I was a child, millions a year.

There's a site about Japan, I'll try to find it for you. The country has gone insane.

Japanese-American: I'm not sure how to answer your question about the "comfort women" [Korean women allegedly forced into prostitution by and for the Japanese army]. Lots of countries used them, France did during WWI. I believe Italy had something similar too from reading Hemingway's *A Farewell to Arms* – one of the characters always visited the whore house. I also read that there were such programs in Vietnam. They're basically military prostitutes, and it's not only Koreans, there were plenty of Japanese too. Some girls claimed they were kidnapped and forced into the program by the Japanese government. I can't give you any books to read since they're all in Japanese, but basically there's no proof that the government ever did such a thing. All the stories brought to the Japanese Supreme Court have been proven false, with the Korean admitting she was lying and was pressured by her family or whatever to do so. It's possible that some women were forced into prostitution by disorderly soldiers, but those are just stray events. Not one story has been proven. You and I could probably make up stories that we were forced into the comfort women thing, and the Korean press would pick it up and publish it as fact immediately.

Carlos W. Porter: Thanks, I'm glad to know that. It's very interesting to know that these stories have gone before the Supreme Court of Japan.

ON REPUBLICS

Japanese-American: That's a very good point you bring up; how republics degenerate into democracies and then to mob rule and dictatorship.

Carlos W. Porter: Republics are based on a limited franchise, but there is constant pressure to extend the franchise. This has happened in all republics in history. All the original Founding Fathers felt this way about republics, so did the Confederates. Particularly John C Calhoun (OK, he died in 1850, but same difference). No reputable government ever believed in universal suffrage, because it means mob rule, which means dictatorship, i.e., Clinton or Bush.

They did away with the Emperor (personified by Caesar Augustus, who possessed actually rather limited powers) in favour of a Republic and this degenerated into democracy and mob rule. There is only one form of government, and that is authority, preferably somewhat limited authority, but authority. I think this means hereditary monarchy, but that is lost and gone forever, oh my darling Clementine. In Japan obviously the Mikado was best, Shintoism and Buddhism and all that.

Japanese-American: Dictatorships are more honest, you're absolutely correct about that. I hate all this deceit, it makes me sick. It's degrading; completely screws the human mind over.

But I think your article is completely right, democracy today is useless. The government is using it against us and the people don't even know it.

Carlos W. Porter: I don't wish to imply that dictatorship is ipso facto better; I merely mean that there is not much difference, and that dictatorship is more honest. Most traditional dictators (Batista, Santa

Anna, etc.) are like Clinton or Bush, mediocre crooks, with the few rare men of ability (Franco, Salazar). Porfirio Díaz of Mexico was a mixture: a man of great ability who became corrupt later (if the allegations are true; in exchange for modernizing the country, he made extensive land grants to foreign corporations, and these land grants became extremely valuable, while the Catholic Church owned 25% of the rest of the land). But in an emergency, the person with the greatest degree of obviously proven ability will be given more and more power until it is too late – if it becomes obvious that he doesn't have as much ability as people thought he had. The proof of the pudding is in the eating. There are very few men of integrity and ability in any system. That is the problem. There have been hundreds of imitations of the American Constitution, but the men of ability and integrity (like the Founding Fathers) were lacking.

To me, democracy is an ideology, like Communism or Christianity. In the Greek city states, it always failed. It was considered a completely discredited form of government until recently. Even the Founding Fathers never spoke of democracy; they were aristocrats and spoke of a republic. But republics degenerate into democracies, and then into mob rule and dictatorship. Most of the original founders hated democracy and were all disillusioned by 1820 or so, those that were still alive. The Roman Empire went through all these stages as well. Democracy has also always been associated with communism (small c) because of the leveling instinct, everybody is the "same", or supposedly, so in the end, logically, they should all have the same possessions, income and social position.

Whatever form of government is traditional and organic, in my opinion, is best for any people. There's no universal rule as far as I can tell.

ON TERRORISM AND
THE FINE ART OF BOMB-MAKING

Japanese-American: I love how you describe terrorism, couldn't agree more with you. I'm not really sure what a "dirty bomb" is. Does such a thing really exist?

Carlos W. Porter: A dirty bomb is an atomic bomb which releases larger than normal amounts of radiation. OK, so where do you get the plutonium? I once read a website about how to make bombs, and let me tell you something, if anybody ever tries to bomb you, you better hope he got his info off the Internet because anybody who does is probably 1000 times more dangerous to himself than anybody else. It was *The Anarchist's Cookbook*, easily available in book form.

The fine art of bomb-making off the Internet is an oft-touted excuse for the censorship of this medium. As we shall soon see, there is no such danger.

Cela n'existe pas, monsieur.

Anyway, in a book, you start at the beginning, and at the beginning – maybe page 3 – it says this stuff should only be made by experienced chemists with full laboratory equipment, proper ventilation, etc. etc., all sorts of safety warnings, so you click on a link at random and start on page 80 and blow yourself up!

For example, you put the cork back in the bottle, BOOM! You forgot to notice that on page 5 or so it told you to clean all surfaces, because the slightest residue can cause an explosion. Also it says never make more than a gram of the stuff (enough to blow up a Coke machine), so you decide to make potassium permanganate in your kitchen without ventilation, without gloves, without clean surfaces, without a respirator and without a protective apron, by boiling about half a pound of salt substitute which you bought in a dietary store. BOOM!

The only bombers you really have to worry about are the ones working for the government. Most bombers are experienced or professional chemists working in teams with professional electronics technicians (for example, TV repairmen). Of course these people don't need the Internet. So how the hell is a street thug like Padilla [Chicago gang leader tortured by the US government for years, destroying his mind, for allegedly planning to manufacture a "dirty bomb"] going to make an atomic bomb?

Most bombers blow themselves up because the detonators and timers are defective because they are old, stolen, bought on the black market and/or constructed by amateurs. That's the reason for suicide bombing: no need for a detonator or timer. Most explosive mixtures are so sensitive that just putting the cork back in a small bottle can kill you. I suspect the Palestinians use mostly dynamite, which is very stable, with a friction trip-wire detonator. No timer.

The whole story about Padilla makes me laugh. Why not accuse him of sending all those anthrax letters a few years back? Padilla is undoubtedly a criminal, but how the hell is he going to make an atomic bomb, dirty or clean? Crack, maybe, but hell, any whiz-kid physics student can make an atomic bomb; in theory, the problem is getting the plutonium and then detonating the device before you die of radiation sickness. So really...

America has never been threatened by a foreign enemy since the War of 1812 (when the British burnt Washington). All our enemies are of our own creation: Japan, Communism, etc. now the goddamn Moslems. How the hell can Moslems do us any harm unless they are allowed to immigrate in large numbers? In Algeria, you could be walking down the street, and presto! An Arab cuts your throat from behind and disappears into the crowd, it only takes them a second. Remember they've all been slaughtering animals since they were kids, they know how. They don't need dirty bombs and hijacked planes. If these people are a problem, we have only ourselves to blame.

And where terrorism is concerned, hell, a kid can wreck a train. Can you imagine thousands of kids tossing rocks on cars from bridges, etc. etc.? It doesn't take much to disrupt modern civilization, so why invite them over by the billions and then antagonize them? I haven't heard of one serious crime committed in the United States by an Arab, in Europe, everywhere else, yes, gang rapes, car theft, shoplifting, etc. drug dealing, but terrorism? No. OK, a few cases in France, one or two in Spain. They don't even rob banks. So terrorism?

Plus all you need to do is rent an apartment next to an airport with a high-powered rifle or other weapon equipped with incendiary bullets, and you can kill 200 people just like that, while the plane is getting ready to take off or has just landed. Nobody needs to hijack a plane. Also, when the hell did the Arabs ever have the A-bomb? All they've got is home-made junk, made from our artillery shells. The USSR exploded an atomic bomb in 1949 and we never did a goddamn thing. We continued to trade with them, gave them foreign aid, 80 billion bucks in loans.

Americans are nuts. I get stuff from Human Events, conservatives, they support Bush, they've got to suffer a lot before they see any sense at all.

When the Jews run America into the ground completely, then maybe people will see some sense. But I don't think so. The only thing you can hope for is a dictator with ability. Essentially, there's no difference politically between the USA and the People's Republic of the Congo.

ON FASCISM

Japanese-American: I see what you mean now when you say all dictators follow the same policies on centralization, industrialization, protectionism; whereas Mussolini used the state to achieve these means, Hitler used the race. So how does one support fascism but reject communism at the same time if both are founded on similar ideas? Where do you think one should place the limit on the power of the state?

Carlos W. Porter: Frankly, on necessity; depends on the circumstances. Desperate ills call for desperate remedies.

Hitler I think was the most coherent and the most realistic of all modern statesmen. The two extremes are the Confederacy and National Socialism. They have many things in common, but I think really they were opposites. Hitler said there is no freedom to sin against the race and hence posterity. That was his standard. The power of the state was a means to an end.

Also, you can choose between similar systems of ideas if one is better than the other, more intelligent, better planned, more realistic. To me National Socialism was the ultimate in realism, but people don't understand it. Communism of course was not realistic at all and its leaders were incompetent at everything except plotting.

ON THE CONFEDERACY

Japanese-American: Definitely to some extent Lincoln was a dictator; suspending habeas corpus, dictating Congress, expanding national power, etc. But he's an amateur compared to Stalin and Mao. In some aspects I sympathize with the South because of their similarities with Japan. Both had very committed soldiers, allegations over POW abuses, traditional cultures, absolute occupations, military tribunals, incinerated cities, etc. Also both were provoked economically by the Union into war, both were fighting for their national sovereignty, and had exaggerated tales of atrocities.

Carlos W. Porter: I appreciate your comments on the Confederacy more than I can tell you. Coming from a Japanese-American this means more than I can say. I think the Confederates were among the only Americans who ever had a real sense of honor and decency. I always thought of them as samurai, knights of war, myself.

I don't believe that everybody should be the same or that different countries should imitate each other. There is room for the ethnic identity of every racial and national group, but only with a reasonable degree of independence (politically and geographically) and mutual respect.

CONCLUSION

I do not believe in unilateral masochism on one side and unilateral victimization on the other, but I think we should recognize the truth about past events by studying revisionist history instead of wartime propaganda; we should look inside ourselves and admit that our enemies are not the only ones who have done wrong. I believe this is in accordance with the tenants of all the world's religions. This is the importance of revisionism.

We don't need to pay reparations in money to the descendants of people who died centuries ago, but we should examine history with a bit of objectivity and humility. This cannot be done without an objective study of history. For example, we do not need the Japanese to "apologize" for attacking Pearl Harbor or China, but we need to understand why they did so.

I also believe that reparations and forgiveness do not boil down to simply handing over taxpayer's cash, or the cash of a few tax-free foundations or corporations in search of tax write-offs and PR. I recommend the book *The Forced War* for a study as to Hitler's methods; in reality he was the greatest conciliator who ever lived; a man who truly "turned the other cheek", even in wartime, until he was forced to fight back. A politician seeks to satisfy his followers; a statesman seeks to satisfy his enemies, so that he can reach an agreement with them. This is what Hitler attempted to do. Everything else is propaganda. I believe that the Japanese attempted to do the same thing, with both China and the US. They fought because they had to.

After building up Communism for 80 years and handing over all the colonial empires to them, creating chaos everywhere, particularly Africa and China, after allowing the Communists to steal and develop the atomic bomb for 50 years, all this talk about Iraq is simply ridiculous.

Carlos W. Porter,
September-October 2004.

FROM A FORMER U.S. INTELLIGENCE OFFICER ON IRMA GRESE

Dear Mr. Porter,
 I have read with great interest your writings on the trial and execution of Irma Grese. [The articles were written by Joe Belling. – Carlos W. Porter.] I do not agree with everything that you say in your writings but I must admit that you make some very compelling arguments and I applaud you for both demonstrating the poor evidence leading to Fräulein Grese's conviction and your courage to do so. As I read I actually felt sick that a young girl could possibly have been executed in error. I am a former career US Military Officer who served both in the US Army and Navy. I worked for several years in the intelligence arena and I know from personal experience that military prosecutors can twist offenses to appear to be much worse than they really are. I also know, as a former military officer, that she could not possibly have had the responsibility and authority claimed by the Jewish "witnesses." No military in the world would be effective with 19 and 20 year olds carrying on as she has been accused, and clearly the SS would have been one of the more disciplined branches in the world!!! If Fräulein Grese had actually sent thousands to their deaths (or even 100... or perhaps even 10) would she have stayed in the camps until the end and risked being captured and identified? It seems that a reasonable person who would have committed those crimes would have seen that the end was coming and would have made a quick break for freedom. I have little doubt that Fräulein Grese was a postwar victim in the wrong place at the wrong time.
 ...As a former intelligence officer I still need to be careful.
 ...I do not agree with your political position. But I do think that much of what you write about the post war trials may very well be true. Isn't it obvious that the victor always writes the history? As I said, I am not in agreement with "everything" you say but I do believe the truth resides somewhere between what we have been taught to believe (as the victor writes) and what you have demonstrated in your own writings.
 I don't know what else to say. I have felt sick after reading what you said about Irma Grese. I wish that it could somehow be corrected but obviously it cannot. I do hope that God shows mercy to those who

have been unjustly convicted and executed and that he holds the perpetrators responsible.

...Just as a point of interest. I personally saw an individual accused of some minor crimes. The military prosecutors embellished these accusations into something much more than they were originally meant to be. The prosecutor also included many other charges other than the original, nearly all of which were probably rumors. During the course of these events the individual in question, probably for his own amusement, started a new rumor about something he supposedly did. He made it up... it was a complete fabrication. Within a month, this "rumor" became an official part of the prosecutors charge list... even though the defendant made it up. This means that the prosecutor was not interested in truth and could not possibly have had a witness, and was quite willing to include rumor to the detriment of the defendant. I am sure that something like this happened to Irma Grese and probably others.

Reading this kind of thing, about Grese, actually makes me angry. It would be nice if there was a way to really sort through all of this and determine the truth.

Regards,
[Name withheld].
January 13, 2006.

[COMMENT: Grese's real mistake, and probably her only real crime, was failing to smile in most of her photographs. Would you smile in her position? Actually, when she did smile, they used that against her, too: they said she felt "no remorse". – Carlos W. Porter.]

www.ingramcontent.com/pod-product-compliance
Lightning Source LLC
LaVergne TN
LVHW041544060526
838200LV00037B/1137